D0373436

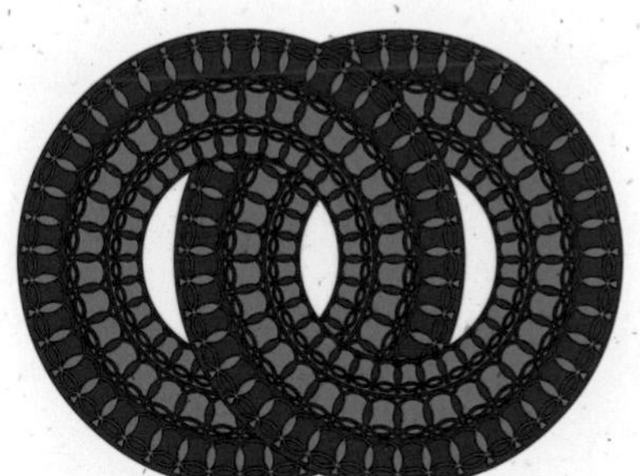

ELEGY FOR THE FLOATER

March 8, 2008

To Bert and Susan,
With regards,
Teresa

ELEGY FOR THE FLOATER

Teresa Carson

TERESA CARSON

FOREWORD BY THOMAS LUX

CavanKerry Press LTD.

CavanKerry Press Ltd.
Fort Lee, New Jersey
www.cavankerrypress.org

Library of Congress Cataloging-in-Publication Data

Carson, Teresa, 1954–
Elegy for the floater / Teresa Carson. – 1st ed.
p. cm.
ISBN-13: 978-1-933880-07-5
ISBN-10: 1-933880-07-4
I. Title.

PS3603.A7763E44 2007
811'.6–dc22

2007043458

Cover art, Pontiac in Meadows, Tim Daly © 2007
Author photograph by Miriam Berkley
Cover and book design by Peter Cusack

First Edition 2008
Printed in the United States of America

LaurelBooks

Elegy for the Floater is the fifth title of CavanKerry's Literature of Illness imprint. *LaurelBooks* are fine collections of poetry and prose that explore the many poignant issues associated with confronting serious physical and/or psychological illness.

CavanKerry is grateful to the Arnold P. Gold Foundation for the Advancement of Humanism in Medicine for joining us in sponsoring this imprint. Offering LaurelBooks as teaching tools to medical schools is the result of shared concerns—humanism, community, and meeting the needs of the underserved. Together with the Gold Foundation, CavanKerry's two outreach efforts, *GiftBooks* and *Presenting Poetry & Prose*, bring complimentary books and readings to the medical community at major hospitals across the United States.

The Arnold P. Gold Foundation

CavanKerry Press is grateful for the support it receives from the New Jersey State Council on the Arts.

Acknowledgments

Some of these poems, or earlier versions of them, appeared in the following journals:

Calyx: "To My Mother Waiting on 10/01/54"
Lumina: " A Note to My Future Biographer"
Psychoanalytic Perspectives: "The History of My Nightmares"

"The First Signs of Spring" was included in *The Breath of Parted Lips: Voices from the Robert Frost Place*, Volume 2 (CavanKerry Press, 2004).

Thanks to my teachers: Howard Levy, Stephen Dobyns, Suzanne Gardinier, Joan Larkin.
Thanks to my fellow students at Sarah Lawrence College: Holly Posner, Michael Carman, Dulcy Brainard.
Thanks to my friends: Evelyn Ripp, Kathleen McQuaide, Robin Leone, Cynthia Flacks, Jack Wiler.

Special thanks to the three people who made this book possible:
Joan Cusack Handler, who—from the very beginning—believed in, encouraged, and supported my voice and me.
Tom Lux, who opened the door and welcomed me into the MFA program at Sarah Lawrence College.
Dr. Rivka Greenberg, who—by listening, listening, listening—helped me to find a way out of silence.

And thanks beyond thanks to my husband, John, whose love makes everything possible.

Viola: What country, friends, is this?
Captain: This is Illyria, lady.
Viola: And what should I do in Illyria?
My brother he is in Elysium.
Perchance he is not drown'd: what think you, sailors?
Captain: It is perchance that you yourself were saved.
Viola: O my poor brother!—and so perchance may he be.

—William Shakespeare, *Twelfth Night*

Contents

Breakup

The Art of Restoration

The Road to the River Blocked

FAMILIES

Families. Most readers know Tolstoy's famous statement about families and novels, which goes something like this: all happy families are happy in the same way and all unhappy families are unhappy in different ways and that's why we don't write novels about happy families. We have our Cleaver families on TV but not often in our best books. Herein lies the power and originality of Teresa Carson's *Elegy for the Floater*.

Autobiographical poems (or memoirs, novels) are nothing new, however. We are living in an age of memoir and have been for well over a decade and it seems not to be letting up. There are dangers in writing autobiographically. One danger might be ending up classified as a member of a group of writers/poets who become known as the ME, NO, ME, NO, MEEEE! School, a footnote re: a number of writers who straddled a millennia. A greater danger to autobiographical writing, I believe, is this: in most of it the speaker, the protagonist, the "I" ends up, no matter what kind of hell they've been through, smelling like a rose. But: it's perfectly normal, human, and even necessary to tell our own stories. I'm wary of the above—let's call the first self-indulgence and the second self-congratulation. They seem to me to be traps that can make it easier to delude ourselves (I said we're human!), but they are traps Teresa Carson never falls into. At times she even seems to be mocking those traps.

These poems can be harrowing. Ten children, two troubled parents. The speaker's own excesses and catastrophes (remember: a lot of the time frame of this book is the 1970s!) but always the author's relentless honesty, clarity, understatement, humor, and skill keep the poems from tipping into the abyss of self-pity.

As I said, there are a lot of people in these poems, a family of twelve and then several ancillary characters. The prime characters, however, are the mother, father, and the speaker. As the book (I almost said poem—this book is really one long poem) reaches its final sequence, a brilliant crown of sonnets, its most important character, the speaker's brother, who died a suicide, by drowning, fully emerges. The strictness of the form is never obtrusive—it just does its job, which is to give a frame, a tension, something for the powerful emotion to work off of or against, and thus increasing its tension, its powerful sentiment.

Some years ago I was writing a nonfiction article about a bridge in San Diego, California, that was a popular spot for suicide attempts. I was interviewing one of the bridge workers whose job it was to try to recover bodies after someone had jumped. She said what she always hoped for was "a floater." I thought this an insensitive term, at first. But she went on: "If we can recover the body before the currents take it out to sea, then we at least have something we can give the family, for a proper burial, or some kind of closure."

By writing this book, and by ending it (but for a short coda) with the crown of sonnets, Teresa Carson has rescued her family (as much as a family can be rescued) and rescued her brother (as much as the drowned can be rescued). That a book of poems can do this is a miracle. For which I am grateful.

—Thomas Lux
Atlanta
December 2007

SUICIDE

Mors voluntaria, or suicide, is more common than most people think. It is the third leading cause of death for Americans age fifteen to twenty-four, and remains a significant cause of death in all age groups. It is estimated that nearly one million people worldwide take their own lives every year. As disheartening as this statistic is, it actually belies the profound effect of suicide. If each of those people has even just a handful of family, friends, coworkers, neighbors, it can quickly be appreciated how vast a net suicide casts. The effects of suicide on those left behind—as Teresa Carson eloquently conveys in her poems—are complicated, tortuous, and lasting. On a larger scale, one can appreciate how suicide penetrates our society with deep, tenacious tendrils.

In my medical clinic and in the hospital wards, I see many patients whose lives have been affected by suicide. These deaths remain as thorns in their souls, continually pricking at their emotional well-being. For me, personally, the two decades since my earliest childhood friend took his life have done little to damp the painful memories. I carry this recollection with me, and it informs the interaction with my patients. As I walk the halls of my hospital and the streets of my city, I see the sweet child that he was, the perplexed adolescent that he grew into, the depressed young adult that he became . . . and then I'm left with the aching thoughts of the mature adult that he never had the opportunity to become. I mourn the friend that I have not been able to grow old with, and the ineradicable wound his family lives with.

The pain of depression, and the drive of some people with depression to end that pain are sensations that many of us have difficulty comprehending. Anita Darcel Taylor, in her essay "By My Own Hand," wrote: "I have no grand wish for death. I do not view suicide as a desire to end life or a dramatic way to go down in flames. Rather, it is a tool in my possession—the only one, really—that offers a permanent end to my pain. When I have lost enough of myself to this disease as to become unrecognizable even to me, I will stop. I will go no further. That, I tell myself, is my earned choice."

I have pondered these words many times. The clinician in me wants to insist that with the right tools—therapy, medications, support systems—most depressions can be treated, at least enough to pull someone back from the harrowing brink. But the reality, sadly, is that our tools are often no match for the fury of depression. I'm not ready to give up hope, or to stop trying. I will continue to assiduously treat my patients' mental illnesses, but I remain humbled by the fact that, even with the best of medical science, we will be only successful in part. And that is when I will turn to literature, to poetry like Teresa Carson's, to fill in the other part.

Danielle Ofri, MD, PhD, D. Litt (hon)
Assistant Professor of Medicine
NYU School of Medicine
Editor in Chief, *Bellevue Literary Review*

WISDOM

I love the written word; yet I rarely read poetry. It was always the really smart kids who seemed to understand it; I enjoyed the rhythm—some of the images—but I could never quite shake the feeling that poetry is smarter than me. Poetry intimidated me. So I was somewhat reluctant to write the foreword for this book.

Until I read these poems. And I was mesmerized. You see, I do know trauma and loss and pain; and I do know the empty spaces in the hearts of young children who have been humiliated, ignored, degraded—injured by word and hand. And I do know heroism and courage and wisdom when I see it in the maltreated grown old. These words—these poems—convey with beauty and power the emotions that pour from loss, love, trauma, reconciliation and healing. In my work it is often so difficult to show someone who has not experienced loss or trauma the complexity and the intensity of these experiences; it is difficult in an academic article or a clinical process to capture the full measure of what it is we seek to heal. And because of that, many are ineffective as clinicians; they are insensitive, disconnected and non-empathic. This only replicates the empty and painful relationships of the patient and compounds their pain. But in these words—these sometimes raw, sometimes funny, always powerful poems—one can connect to a fragment of the pain, and hope, of Teresa Carson. A moment of clarity; an image; a sensation evoked from her words can teach. And these poems will teach anyone who takes the time to read these gifts. I'm no longer afraid of poetry.

And I am grateful for the opportunity to read these poems; and thankful for the courage of Teresa Carson. The price of the wisdom that comes from the adversity of life is high; loneliness, sadness, despair, anxiety, self-loathing and a host of other negative emotions weave the tapestry of this wisdom. Teresa

Carson is wise. She shares her wisdom in this remarkable book. Thank you for your life, Teresa Carson. Thank you for your words.

With great respect, admiration and gratitude,

—Bruce D. Perry, MD, PhD
Senior Fellow
The Child Trauma Academy
Houston, TX
November 8, 2007

ELEGY FOR THE FLOATER

Elegy for the Floater

Yet again? What do you here? Shall we give
o'er and drown? Have you a mind to sink?

—William Shakespeare

The barking boy

lurches across the rain-slick street—
no umbrella. Snorts as he slaps his cheeks.
I cross to avoid him.
Sticks his hands in gutter water,
picks out a crushed cup,
throws it like a girl
and lets loose with a louder bark
when it falls short of his target—
a boy near his age cycling away from us.
The barking boy sees me.
I dip my umbrella so I can't see him.

Retards we called kids like him in the Sixties.
Oversized dumb Walter was one—
I hated him when Sister Grace's class
saw him give me a chocolate heart.
And greasy Alice wearing Goodwill clothes,
and Mary Ann chewing her arm
instead of giving the knee-jerk YES
when Sister Malachy grilled us one by one,
Do you believe in God?
Freaks, rejects, barkers all.

The barking boy kicks off a shoe.
It thunks the door of a passing car.

The barking boy will become the man
who marches down Broad Street screaming,
I don't want to, over and over;

who runs into LaBella Deli at lunch
cursing in every direction;
who, as my brother Joseph did,
carries dog shit in his pockets,
walks backwards through his mother's rooms,
wears a flannel shirt and shoes with holes the July night
when he wraps chains and cement blocks around his chest
and jumps off the Turnpike bridge.

Someday the barking boy's sister
will sit in a police station
across the desk from Detective Nankivell
who will hand her an autopsy report
and three Polaroids of *human remains,*
which she won't look at because
she wants to appear reasonable,
to make sure this detective,
everyone in the station, in Kearny, in the world,
knows she is not
a barker.

Fill in the [Blanks] for July 3–25, 1986

During his last appointment with
the psychiatrist who prescribed the five
antipsychotic drugs—which he took
on a [time interval] basis—Joe asks [words].
Dr. Castillo replies [words].

I don't attend my brother Tom's wedding,
because a feud over [reason] has split
my siblings into non-speaking factions,
but Joe does and he's in a [adjective] mood.

Forty-two-year-old, 6'1" & 140 pounds Joe,
who doesn't drive, manages to haul 91 pounds
of cinder blocks and steel chains eight miles from Jersey City
to [location] near the Passaic River by [details of process].

A pleasure boat captain spots something
floating in the river. He feels [adjective] when he realizes
what it is. Fire Boat #1 recovers an Unknown Male.
Possible [crime type] says Det. Nankivell.
That afternoon, while someone cuts one chain from
the subject's body, I'm at work, [present participle verb],
and Joe hasn't even crossed my mind in [time interval].

Autopsy Report

A possible ID in the pocket
which is wet and dirty and undecipherable
at this time.

The chain had been padlocked
around the neck and waist and chest regions,
however, hands and feet were free.

The body was placed in a wastebasket.
The cinder blocks were freed
after cutting the chain. Keys found
in the pocket fit the locks.

The Doctor also stated the deceased was
distraught over the death of his mother
who died 2-18-86.

In shirt pocket: prescription for
#1 Prolixin Hydrochloride
#2 Inderal
#3 Cogentin
#4 (scored out)
#5 Chloral Hydrate

The socks are well worn.
The shoes have holes in the heels.
Located within the two thighs and from inside
the underwear is removed dead fish.
Earlobes are partially eaten off.

December 1985: While driving on
Bergen Ave. I saw him—head bent
against the cold—but didn't stop.

He worshipped Houdini and retold
the stories of his most famous feats.
Especially the Chinese Water Torture Cell.

When I visited him at Meadowview
he ignored the shouting patient,
who paced close to where we sat,
and said: Don't come here again.

He slept in Mom's bed after she died.

At her wake he sat in a corner
dressed in clean burgundy corduroy
pants and a flannel shirt that was
baggy on his near-skeletal frame.
He held his arms down but couldn't
stop the Prolixin-caused shakes.

When I told him how no one
in the family liked my house because
it was plain he said: I like it;
it's a classic wood-frame
working-class house.

No identifying scars, tattoos or deformities
noted at this point in time.

Set of inked prints of recovered body (John Doe).
Note: due to decomp there is no better set avail,
however fingers are available. (Exhibit A)

Above subject (victim) is a mental patient.

He taught me to make kites from
rice paper, balsa, electric blue paint.

What do I have to remember him
by? Two books he gave me (Keats,
The Bestiary), one black&white
photo—a profile shot.

The nurse at Medical Center:
Miss, your brother cannot have matches.

Weights and Measures

Note: All weights in grams unless otherwise noted.

White jockey shorts:	Size 34
Brain matter (semiliquid & gooey):	1276
Right lung:	472.8
Left lung:	403.4
Cinder block #1:	41 lbs.
Cinder block #2:	43 lbs.
Body (estimated by pathologist):	190 lbs.
Body (estimated by me, based on last time I saw him—at Al's Diner—alive):	140 lbs.
Liver:	988.8
Spleen:	50
2 chains, 3 locks (1 yellow Guard Security & 2 silver metal):	7 lbs.
Heart:	248.9

Stop

Everything I've told you about Joe's suicide
has been slanted—to make you feel sorry for me
not him.

Look. Someone with *chronic psychophrania,*
even if he takes the drugs—which Joe stopped
doing because he hated the side effects—is tough
to be around. He stank, saved bottles of pee,
kept getting arrested, gave incoherent speeches
in court. When Mom was near death he unplugged her phone.
I'd rush over when no one answered and find him sitting
in the kitchen, playing guitar.

Listen. Three months before his death we met
at Al's Diner for lunch. He looked like he slept
under cardboard, on subway grates.
The waitress showed us to a back booth. I saw
heads turn, imagined whispers and finger-points.
My whole life spent trying to blend in, to shake off
the ghost of Mom's mental illness and here he was—
his sickness displayed for everyone to see.

Listen closer. I loved my remembered Joe,
not the wreck across the table who just hadn't tried hard enough
to break from our past.

Listen even closer. I have to whisper this part:
his death was a relief.

The History of My Nightmares

Their tales are full of sorcerers and ogres
Because their lives are.

—Randall Jarrell

To My Mother Waiting on 10/01/54

That October might have begun
pretty much like this one. Last night,
first chilly night, we shut all the windows,
the cat curled between John's legs, I slept
with a blanket over my head. At six a.m., wrapped
in a sweater, I checked the newly dug
beds of bulbs—tulips, your favorite—
and wondered if they, and the ones I planted
on your grave, would survive the months
of frozen ground.

You were three days from bearing your tenth;
rather than risk a fall, going up and down
two steep flights, you stayed inside.
At six a.m. you may've been in your rocking chair,
half-listening for fights over blankets
or Pop's return from the graveyard shift
while you folded, again, a newly washed stack
of secondhand diapers and tees.
Maybe a draft made you shiver or a pain
made you think *it's beginning.*

Too soon the cold will kill the last blooms
on asters, hydrangea, Autumn Joy sedum.
Too soon another breakdown
left you in the depression that lasted
the rest of your life. Too soon Judge Grossi ruled
you were *dangerous to your child's welfare.*
At fifteen I was free to leave.

But this morning, I went back to when
the cold hadn't yet settled in,
when you were waiting for me.

Webs

my mother drew spider webs
on any paper within her reach

my mother on the telephone
drew webs across names in our address book

my mother in her rocker
drew webs on bills and Christmas cards

my mother in my bedroom drew
webs deep in diaries

everywhere in that house I found
ink   pencil   crayon

My Mother Said

I was sure you liked butter pecan. Then I'll have to eat it all myself.
I was sure you liked *Harlequins*.
I was sure you liked *The Sound of Music*, lamb, the color green.
You can't be hungry.
There's none left and you had enough.
It's nothing, your knee's not broken, the bleeding will stop.
Dry your hair in the oven.
You're making too much noise, you'll wake the dead.
Hold it in.
You're really not angry/sad/happy/or scared, you're overtired/run-down/or sick.
You don't know what you're talking about.
You don't mean that.
G+ in Reading? I never got less than E+.
God sees everything. Do you want to burn in hell?
Stop showing off.
Mary's the Writer. Vin the Math Wiz. Joan the Teacher. Anne the Artist. Tom the Scientist. John the Athlete. Louise the Beauty. Joe the Genius.
You're the Baby.
Stop fidgeting—how can I sleep when you won't stay still.
Tonight go sleep in VinMaryJoanJoeAnneLouiseJohnTom's old bed.
If you miss Pop so much, go sleep in his bed.
Who told you that?
Good girls wear socks not stockings.
Good girls wear skirts not pants.
SSSSHHHH. Don't say that.
I don't care if it's 1964 and no one around here wears summer gloves. A lady wears gloves whenever she goes out. The gloves are both white, that's all that counts.

Why of course you're pretty enough to be a model, and you haven't finished
growing.
Your brother or sister is, has, did, can, would always or would never.
I'll read your diary whenever I want.
You don't need a skin doctor—I had bad skin when I was your age and
look at my skin now.
I thought you were smarter than that.
I thought you knew better than that.
Nine kids and not one priest or nun—you're my last hope.
Of course it's OK you quit, Honeybunch—it takes too much to be a ______.
You're embarrassing yourself.
How dare you tell her our business?
I heard what you said on the phone.
Don't act smart.
Don't get up, I'll get it for you in a few minutes.
What if I tell Sister Eymard what her *class monitor* did?
You don't want to play with Vita, her mother lets those kids run wild and
they're Italian.
It's OK to tell me what your brothers and sisters say behind that door.
I'll have the men come and take you away.
It can't be too small because it's your size, it's a pretty dress, and I'm not
going back to Gimbels.
I'll stuff paper in the toes and then they'll fit.
Get your head out of the clouds.
That didn't happen.
That couldn't happen.
No girls underpants in the drawer? Wear your brother's.
Why are you having a tantrum—I'm sure he didn't mean to cut off Herbie-
the-hippo's ears and tail.
So what if it's Midge not Barbie,
it's what was left.
Pop wouldn't give me money,

you're lucky you got anything,
who do you think you are,
you want and want, don't you,
you're not the only one around here.
I wanted to teach but had to leave Hunter to care for my mother and then I had all of you.
There's nothing I would change.
Do you think you could do better?
Money doesn't grow on trees.
You're breaking my heart.

But most of the time
she said nothing.

First Communion Day

We didn't own a camera.
Mr. Shea, our downstairs neighbor,
offered to take these two
black-and-white snapshots
outside 111 Belmont where
I'd live with Mom and Pop
for eight more years.
Forsythia, past blooming, behind me.
Mom sewed and starched
my plain but glare-white cotton dress.
I, always first in by-size-lines,
enjoyed refusing food
and believed my pleasure came
from acting like
Saint Catherine—too busy
with holy thoughts to eat.
A lopsided, lace-covered hat
monopolized my head. Ribbons tied
in an oversized bow
under my moon-face chin.
Clutched in my right hand
the white plastic pocketbook—
given as part of the sacrament—
which held my new white rosary
and gold-edged children's missal.
I'd already developed
the left-forearm-protecting-midriff pose
which, forty years later, I still
unconsciously use.

In one shot I wear the face that,
adults complained, made me look
too serious for a child.
In the other a tight-lip half-smile,
the result of Mr. Shea's
Give me a smile.
You're pretty when you smile.

Postscript: There's a third snapshot.
Didn't mention it sooner because
I wanted to keep it for myself.
It's of Pop and me.
He's wearing a wrinkled Sunday shirt,
sleeves rolled up, loosened tie.
He's carrying me in his arms
and smiling at me, not the camera.
I'm looking straight at the camera,
my face one big smile;
Mr. Shea didn't have to ask and, yes,
in this one, I'm pretty.

The Library

I knew the route to the Miller Branch
by heart. Once handed a card,
first day of second grade,
I walked there, by myself, twice a week.
In summer, one surefire way
to get out was tell my mom
the library so my weekly trips
increased to four or five.
Otherwise I'd be stuck inside with her.

Six and a half blocks.
One scary spot: tenements past
Communipaw where kids
played wild sidewalk tag.
Women crowded on stoops yelled,
Cut out the noise!
Don't make me smack you!
Stop hitting your sister!
Stay away from the cars!

I kept close to the curb,
eyes dropped, until I reached marble steps
leading to huge glass and oak doors
that opened to the smell of books.
Sneaked by Miss Marino, who
whispered, *Hello, Terry,* if she saw me.
Slipped into the Children's Room.

A mural by the picture books:
children in a rowboat

on a wild sea. No one was coming
to rescue them.

Sometimes I did nothing but pick up
familiar books, hug them, set them back
in their spaces. Sometimes ran
my fingers across rows and rows of spines
then went home empty-handed and told
my mom, *The book I wanted wasn't there.*

Life Everlasting

More times than I care to remember
Mom or a priest or a nun preached to me
that poverty on earth was a blessing because
it gave us a better shot at a rich afterlife.

Thus, I should never want what others had
but, instead, look forward to the treats
God would shower me with when I died.
But despite their insistence that scraping by

was a stroke of luck, I would—given a choice—
have picked the ruffly dress in Pesin's window,
non-pinching shoes, a shelf of dolls, bags
of penny candies, and, oh yeah, enough blankets

to keep me warm through January nights,
enough food to fill my bottomless hungers.

The Edison National Historic Site

Once a year, on what seemed the hottest day,
Pop took me to Edison's West Orange labs.
Science, unlike tigers or art, bored me. Science stank
like the rotten-egg smell Tommy made
with his chemistry set.

But there we were, right after the nine o'clock
Children's Mass, on the 107 bus.
Because it was the Lord's Day,
I wore a clean dress, anklets without holes,
and Mary Janes my mom had polished with butter.
In Newark we changed to the 73. When we were lucky,
we caught it right away. Unlucky days,
Pop gave me one of two peanut-butter sandwiches
from a brown paper bag.

By noon we followed Park Ranger Bob
into Building Two, past benches cluttered
with beakers, pipettes, bottles of dried spurge,
milkweed, goldenrod, dogbane.
These bottles, the ranger droned, *hold*
the remains of Edison's efforts to find
a substitute for imported rubber.
In Building Five he praised Edison's *work ethic—*
60, 80, 100 hours per week!
We spent hours in the oak-paneled study.
After the tour left Pop hung back
and pointed out, in case I'd missed anything,
10,000 scientific journals and books,

the rolltop where the Old Man worked through nights,
the couch where he took his famous naps,
and the clock that stopped at the hour of his death.

Standing for hours, hunger, heat,
and smells jumbled my stomach.
I wasn't listening when Pop said,
Edison was self-made—
no schooling, no bucks, no help from his family.

His tone said, *This is important, listen,*
ask questions, but getting through the bus ride
without throwing up took everything I had.

Later, as we hurried the six blocks
from bus stop to home, fresh air
fixed my stomach and I wanted
to ask about Edison, but could tell,
from the way he pulled me along, his mind
was somewhere else—better not bother him.

Summer 1969

Mom sank further into her silence. I rode PATH
to Ninth Street and joined runaways who squatted
in Lower East Side buildings, panhandled
by subway stairs, walked barefoot on hot sidewalks.
I collapsed in laughter in front of Balducci's after smoking
too much hash—*This stuff isn't working*—when it hit:
my legs gave out. Discovered Night Train and Bali Hai.
Snuck backstage at the Fillmore but never met Joplin, my Queen.
Popped Black Beauties because I wanted to stay
long past the end of every party. Chanted *Time to Pick Up the Gun,*
Power to the People, Make Love Not War—that last one
already passé. Rain-danced in Washington Square's fountain.
Enjoyed my first French kiss and breast-squeeze
from Sunshine, a nickel-bag dealer who gave me pot.

Kathy 1969

We met protesting the sale of California grapes
at Fine Fare on Bleecker. She carried her life
in a knapsack. Her lover sold, to tourists,
crepe-paper poppies. He was older—late twenties—
had long curly hair, flirted with women
until they bought, teased me about my age,
nicknamed me *Cherry*.
She took me to his place.
His pregnant wife out—a doctor's appointment.
In case the neighbors spied, two female guests
are less suspicious than one. We sat on the bed,
shared a joint. They wrestled, pulled me into their play.
One minute we were a laughing, twisted pile,
the next she stormed out the door. Fine with me.

Dog Guards Bed

At first I didn't want to leave.
He slid his hand
under my t-shirt, under my bra, his palm rubbed
my crotch, he groaned, *You're making me so hot.*
His hand reached to unzip my jeans.

And then I couldn't.
I pushed his hand
away, jerked up. He slammed me down,
commanded King, *GUARD THE BED!* then explained,
If you try to run, he'll kill you.

Afterwards

He jumped up, turned on TV,
said nothing. He'd forgotten I was there.

I used a kitchen towel
to wipe blood off my thighs.

From behind I put my arms
around his seated form.

The intercom buzzed. His wife headed up.
He barked: *Get out, take the stairs, use the back door.*

I stuffed my underpants
deep in a trash can,
wandered uptown
to my sister's place.
I showered.
No one was home.

What I Remembered

How King, his German shepherd, *stayed*
beside my crumpled underpants
waiting for his master's next command.

Deflowered

Before: I'd never seen a penis and didn't know
the mechanics of sex but girls whispered the *first time*
hurt a lot. After: that pain was one less thing to worry about.
Plus I wasn't *easy*—he forced me—which somehow made
it okay to be somewhat proud over the loss of my *cherry*.
Before: no boys my age paid attention to me
so I stayed quiet when my girlfriends debated
if Patty should let Scott-the-surfer feel her up—
they'd gone out all summer—or what Noni should do
if Gregory W., who had a reputation, tried to park
behind Pershing Field. After: I stayed quiet because
I was *grown-up* and *way beyond* their *Seventeen* magazine questions.
Of course, when my best friend asked, *What does it feel like
to come?* I had no idea what she meant but answered, *Great.*

Tramp

If I lied and said I had nothing to do with Kathy or him
after that day then I'd have to stay silent about the rest of '69 and most of '70.

Silent about when he drove me to Albany—a hash-induced impulse.
First time I stayed in a motel. His cock wouldn't go in, no matter
how much he rammed, because I was *too tight*. He enjoyed telling friends,
in front of me, *Can't believe I paid twenty bucks for that room*
and didn't get laid. That's what I get for bringing a baby.

Silent about the five weeks Kathy lived at my sister's house.
She slept past noon and never looked for apartments or jobs
but kept promising she would until my sister kicked her out.
Or about when Kathy confessed she'd fucked Allen, the boy I loved.
It just happened, she swore. *He showed up at my room. We dropped*
blue-dot. You know how it goes. It didn't mean a thing.

Silent about how my Catholic-school uniform excited him.
He'd pick me up from school, drive to secluded places—like the deserted strip
under the Turnpike extension or woods in Staten Island.
Afterwards he'd drop me off two blocks from Belmont—I didn't tell him
exactly where I lived.

Oh and most silent about the night when Kathy and I drank *Jack*.
When she leaned to kiss me I kissed back but when she lifted
my shirt and licked my breasts I pretended to pass out
and didn't answer her repeated *Teresa?*

Discarded Revisions Two Through Fifteen

~~I never met that man.~~

~~I met him but didn't, in my diary,~~
~~record and frame with stars~~
~~every word he said to me.~~

~~I drew his name inside big hearts~~
~~all over my ninth-grade notebooks~~
~~but didn't go to his place with my friend.~~

~~I went but left when they began~~
~~kissing on the bed.~~

~~I joined them on the bed~~
~~but he didn't start kissing me and ignoring her.~~

~~My friend didn't stomp out.~~

~~I left with her.~~

~~I stayed behind~~
~~but he stopped when I said No even though~~
~~I'd let him squeeze my breasts~~
~~and rub my crotch through jeans.~~

~~He kept going but knew~~
~~I was a *cherry* so~~
~~he went gently and slowly.~~

ELEGY FOR THE FLOATER

~~He rammed me,~~
~~who knows how many times,~~
~~but when he finished, when I stood,~~
~~when lines of blood were running down my legs,~~
~~I didn't put my arms around him, didn't buy~~
~~he couldn't stop~~
~~because *I made him hot.*~~

~~I bought his story but went home,~~
~~and told Mom what had happened.~~

~~As usual, I didn't tell Mom anything~~
~~but told at least one sister.~~

~~My mouth didn't stay shut for thirty years~~
~~and I ignored the voice that hissed:~~
~~*A slut, you asked for it,* and *got what you deserved*.~~

~~I kept the rape a secret all my life~~
~~and never challenged what~~
~~that voice inside me said.~~

Kathy 1973

Last time we met: Trenton, Dee-Lite Motel,
Room 14B. Your skin pimpled, eyes dull,
left cheek freshly cut, long sleeves despite
the stifling air. You offered *Jack or joint?*

After your most recent arrest (prostitution,
charge didn't stick) things began looking up.
Your parents took you back, paid for rehab
and steno classes at Katharine Gibbs where

the teachers picked on you, the students were
tight-assed, what else could you do but get stoned?
Then your mom found the bag of used needles
you buried under her prize Carefree Beauties.

The room stank of cat piss, burnt hair, blood.
When you asked, I didn't give my new address.

The History of My Nightmares, 1964–Present

1. Apartment in 111 Belmont

Seven out of nine rooms once used
as bedrooms—one for Mom, for Pop,
the oldest boy, the oldest girl,
and three where kids were doubled up.
Now all but three were empty. Tom claimed
the one with locks. Pop, who stayed
at his girlfriend's place most weekends,
kept the small room off the kitchen.
One hall, two rooms away from his:
Mom's bed. I, age ten, slept next to her,
as I'd done since outgrowing my crib.
But there were no more afternoons I cried
when Pop and Mom went in her room and pushed
the dresser against the door to keep me out.

2. What we did on weekend nights when Pop wasn't home

We didn't own a TV
or radio. We didn't join
the neighbors on the stoop
but three floors up I heard
Mrs. Bybel's gruff voice
telling jokes that made
adults laugh but Mom frown.
I wanted to laugh too.
We said rosaries; the beads clicked
through Mom's fingers.

Prayers blurred to nonwords.
I knelt on the room's east side, she on its west.
Tom stayed behind his closed door. I hoped
my sisters or Joe would show for Sunday dinner.

3. The nightly ritual

Mom got up from her rocking chair,
said, *Time for Tweety-bird and me*
to go to bed, then left the room.
If others were there I lagged a minute
pretending not to care but that meant
I'd have to hurry when halfway down
the hall and out of their sight.
She undressed to her slip. I climbed
in first—my place between wall
and her. She shut the door, turned out
the light, lay down a bodyspace away.
I inched over and snuggled into her side.
She raised her arm and I pressed my face
into breast. No words ever spoken.

4. My collection of nightmares from those years

Rats chewed my toes. Disembodied hands
came up from under the bed and pawed
my stomach. A man on the landing
slipped his hand in the broken panel
and opened the lock. My sister screamed
and screamed. I found dead kittens
in the back of the closet, moldy loaves
in the punched wall, and blood on my pajamas.

The nightmare I'd have for the next thirty years
began: I wake, can't breathe,
something evil at the foot of my bed,
must get away, but paralyzed.
My fingers pull me across the floor,
those deadly hands seconds behind my neck.

5. Night-lights

I couldn't fall asleep—
even in my own bedroom in my own
house—unless there was a light, a bright
light, on in the room.
When staying at hotels or someone's
home, I turned on every light and checked
every corner, at least twice,
before laying down.
And never let myself deep-sleep—
had to stay prepared in case something
happened. What if a killer broke in
and I wasn't awake enough to know?
It's different now: 111 Belmont torn down,
Mom dead, and I sleep soundly next to John.

Breakup

Pain comes from the darkness
And we call it wisdom. It is pain.

—Randall Jarrell

The Last Night I Lived with Mom

I'd been sleeping on the floor
because the minute Pop left—golf
trip with his girlfriend—Mom began,
with Joe's help, moving our furniture,
to three and a half *low-income* rooms
in a rehabbed Harlem tenement;
on the Housing Authority form
she'd signed Pop's name but, in her scheme,
he wasn't going to live there—
just me and Mom, and maybe Joe.

That night she told me: *Pack your stuff,*
we're leaving now. But I was dressed—
sheer peasant blouse, tight jeans—for hanging
at the Square so I said *no.*
The bookcase pushed against the door
kept her out of my room; her fists
demanded *let me in.* A friend
and I, rum-drunk by then, collapsed
in laughs when pious Mom let loose:
YOU GODDAMNED SELFISH WHORE BITCH.

Some minutes later: silence fell,
footsteps backed off. We hurried towards
the stairs but Mom, hiding mid-hall,
flew at my back—*You will do what*
I tell you to—then grabbed a clump
of my hair and, while I struggled, cut
my blouse to pieces with a knife.

She, laughing, ran away, I chased.
I'LL KILL YOU WITH THAT FUCKING KNIFE.
My friend caught up and dragged me out.

In Family Court

1. The Lawyer Preps Me

Don't say a word unless
you're asked a question by the judge.
And keep your answers short—
a *yes* or *no* is best.
Don't look at your mother and don't
react to anything
she says or does—just let
her hang herself. Sit still.
Don't laugh, don't cry, don't frown,
don't make THAT face.

2. What I Said in Court

Yes, when Judge Grossi asked,
You're fifteen years and four months old?

No, when Judge Grossi asked,
Do you want to live with her?

3. What I Heard in Court

The lawyer said *mature*
for age, maintained her grades—
all As in fact—despite
disruptions in home life.

The psychiatrist said *no signs*
of suicidal tendencies.

The social worker said, *Large holes*
in walls, no furniture, unclean,
not much to eat in house,
burns paper in the toilet bowl
to keep the bathroom warm.

The brother-in-law said, *If*
you make her go back there
someone will end up hurt.

The mother said, *You can't*
take her away from me.
This isn't Nazi Germany.

Judge Grossi said, *You're free.*

The father? He didn't say one word.

4. What Happened Then

We were walking to the bus stop.
My sisters, their husbands, and I
were saying *what a victory*
and then I tripped on a crack,
fell down, scraped hands and bloodied knees.
I nodded when they asked *OK?*
but rushed ahead—not wanting them
to see my face or hear me cry.

My Father's Wilderness

Eight months after I left home,
two before my sixteenth birthday.
Pop calls, *Tweety-bird, let's go for a ride.*
I'm outside in minutes.

He drives thirty-five in the left lane on Route 17.
Drivers honk, yell as they pass.
I slump and stay quiet because whatever I say
might send him into a rage and I don't want
our time together ruined.

He takes an unmarked exit,
parks on the shoulder. I light
a cig and follow him
into an overgrown lot.

There's Bendix. He points but I can't see
past weeds and trees. Proud of his job
making *delicate instrumentation*
for warships, planes, rockets, he kept
the box with his jeweler's drills
and the Apollo patch NASA gave him
in his top dresser drawer and showed them
to me many times but didn't invite
any of us, not even Mom, to his retirement dinner.

When I worked days,
I ate lunch here and bird-watched.
We stood in knee-high buzzing weeds.

Bugs flew in my face. Cicadas' clacking
rose and broke above us.

Saw all kinds: finches, sparrows, chickadees,
red-winged blackbirds.
Cardinals nested there one year.
Woodpeckers drilled those holes.
And once, only once, a red-tail
watched me from that branch.
A hawk in Teterboro, Tweety-bird!
He must have lost his way.

I want to tell him,
I miss seeing you every day.
We reach the field's edge.
A bulldozer's parked in a mowed section.

My father stops. *Over there was a mess*
of milkweed. Monarchs loved it.
I light another cig and wonder
how much longer we'll stay here and why
he cares so much about those stupid birds,
keeps calling me *Tweety-bird*, that baby name,
why he let Mom drive me out of our home,
didn't try to stop me from leaving,
and, worst of all, stood on her side in Family Court.

On the way back I stare out the side window.
We don't talk, except twice he asks,
So how are you doing?
Fine, I answer both times.
Good, he says. *Good*.

Since he died, I've tried to find that place,
but the road's changed
and a car wash stands on his lot.

Breakup

—For Ray

By February in Anchorage the hot topic
on everyone's tongue is when and where
the first crack of spring breakup
will appear. Bar pools nail it down to the minute.
Rumored sightings tracked on page one:
Stevens, Ship Creek, Saturday, noon.
Owens, Eklutna, Tuesday, near sunset.

No one wants to miss it,
but the first crack means nothing,
of course. Still to come: bigger cracks,
mudslides, flash floods, people—
misjudging the thickness of ice—drowned.
Their bodies surface in June.

Married three years we went to visit
your Army buds and to check out
Rendez, which started in Gold Rush days—
when trappers and miners hit town
to drink, fuck, fight, do whatever it took
to shake off three months of night.
This one's more civilized—pink-lit
ice castles, an Eskimo blanket toss,
Little Miss Anchorage. Yet locals don't hide
the hunting knives attached to their belts.

The grand finale—a dogsled race—
on a morning with some sun. We borrowed

mukluks to top off layers of clothes
and, unable to bend arms or legs, robot-marched
on packed snow. The muddy race start loud with barks,
commands, loudspeaker jabber. Howling backup dogs,
locked in trucks, stuck their heads out portholes.
A husky dragged a sled loaded with weights.
His owner added more and more until the dog fell
and couldn't get up. When the crowd left
I saw the man cradle the dog in his arms.

Later we drove by hillsides heavy with snow
ready to fall in a flash if we made the sound
that would trigger an avalanche. We slid onto Portage Glacier.
I stopped a few feet in, afraid to go on.
You hiked to its mouth. I lost sight
of your red jacket and the creaking of the blue ice grew
until I feared a line etched on its surface
might split and leave me stranded.
I called *Ray* but my voice didn't carry.
Later you said, *I can't understand your fear.*
The ice is several feet thick. It can't suddenly break.

Back in New Jersey, while we slept, that first crack
of breakup widened.

Lisa at 21

—For Lisa Steinberg, 1981–1987

Always fresh cuts. No one asks why.
Broken mirror, penknife, jagged soup-can top,
but a razor does the trick without much fuss.

June '97: Paradise Truck Stop,
first time she snuck out of a motel room.
Next trucker dropped her in Perryville,
Cookie, on my next haul I'll take you dancing.

'98 North Dakota
'99 & '00 Wyoming
'01 Montana
LuLizzieLauraLindaLee
Now trying *Lisa* again.

At first, in dreams, he showed up every night.
She still hangs chairs on doorknobs,
leaves all lights on, checks behind
and beneath—more than once.
On nights when nothing stops him
she chain-smokes behind the ice machine.

Been in Cowtown nine months now.
Doesn't want to run.
Fast-food joints her job of choice.
Wrinkle-free uniforms—
stains easily scrubbed out in bathroom sink.
Right ways of filling cups,

wrapping foil around burgers,
lifting boxes of fries.
What would you like? What would you like?
The counter between her and them.

Rate for Room 22, Red Wagon Inn: $119.25 per week.
On Fridays she hands cash to paunchy Ken,
who follows her to her room.
You know I love you.
She knows the right laugh to give him.
She knows how to shrink from the hand.

Buys pink roses at Bud's Fill-up.
Been checking out a used Corolla—

Just so happens I'm well-known
for teaching pretty women how to drive.
He takes her to the diner Saturday night.
She leaves as soon as he falls asleep—
but has a story ready just in case.

Under a layer of panties and socks
she keeps a photograph from then:
her at six, clutching Herbie-the-hippo.
I'll come back for you. I swear.

She'd call from pay phones, two a.m.
If he answered, *Lisa is that you?*
she'd say nothing.
If her, she'd whisper,
Why didn't you leave?
Last six times: put coins in the slot,
didn't dial.

Yesterday, when the phone rang,
she dropped burgers on the floor.
Her boss shook his head:
Damn, what a skitty filly!
Gonna take a real man to break you.

To the Man Who Raped a 14-Year-Old Me

I killed you in '95—
malignant lesions
covered your cock
the way my blood once did.

Each second of pain
lasted days. As did mine.
Touch—even the softest—
made you cringe.

Fear fucked you, enjoyed
itself, never left. Did you hate
your body? Good. Did you beg
God to save you?

God didn't. Too bad.
Such an awful way to die.

Phone Installer 1974

As Bill, my union delegate, and Jack,
my boss, and Ken, my boss's boss, explained:
What can we do? They broke the lock because
they felt it wasn't right that you could keep
them out of their john. The law may say
we can't stop girls from taking jobs away
from men, but nothing says we must provide
private facilities. Why waste that kind
of money anyway? We know you'll quit
at the first broken nail. As for your bitch
about the filthy toilets and sinks—
Sweetheart, no one forced you to take this job.
Sure, you can use the Operators' lounge
ten miles away—but go there on your break
or you'll be written up for being AWOL.

Last One to Leave, Turn Out the Lights

Please. Burying them together never sounded like
a great idea, but when we were picking out
Mom's casket at Quinn's, I couldn't bring myself to say:
Let's buy her a separate plot.

After all. How little they even spoke—
except when Pop yelled at her
for some offense (e.g., she bought a duplicate *News,*
which cost all of twenty-five cents).

Furthermore. Did he ever take her to Edison's lab?
Ever call her *Tweety-bird* and *Honeybunch*?
We should have buried her alone.
The second space in his plot should be mine.

But. It's done. I can't remember—does
her casket sit right on top of his?
How many years does it take
for mahogany to rot?

For now I stop by their grave once in a while.
Run-down section. Duncan Projects beyond
the fence. Tonnelle Ave. down the hill. Skyway's
first span rising in the distance.

A Brief History of Gloves

An early example with separate fingers
found on twelfth-century effigy of Henry I,
who, despite his coarse, ill-kept hands,
went ungloved except for state occasions
and hawking.

Mom wore them all the time—
summer, Tuesdays, food shopping.
That's what Ladies did. I hated holding
her mismatched-torn-seams-weird-
stain-on-the-back hand.

An etiquette of the glove existed from
the time of Charlemagne
until the fifteenth century.

What Ladies did. She clung
to one thread: her dad's family branched
from the "Hynes of Troy."

A lover in the fifteenth century paid attention
to subtle meanings in the manipulation
of gloves that might have serious
consequences.

No gloves most childhood winters.
I shaped snow, battled, then pressed
my raw numbness on radiator or stove
door to defrost.

In the fourteenth century gloves treated
with poison were favorite gifts
to one's special enemies.

Gift for my sixteenth birthday: silver-lamé
opera gloves. Years later found in a box.
Silver rubbed off, limp under-glove left.

From the eleventh century on a present
of gloves was a way of recognizing
indebtedness.

My first full-time job. I bought her
a fur-lined buttery leather pair for Christmas.
She lost them by Valentine's Day.

In colonial New England it was customary
to send a pair to relatives and friends
to invite them to a funeral.

We forgot to bring gloves
to Quinn's. Her soft hands, now so thin,
buried bare.

To _____, My One and Only

I.

Many years after Mom's death,
when looking through a box of stuff
taken from her dresser, I find
an envelope addressed to *Mrs. Lamphier.*
It contains eight Valentines—
my father's handwriting—*To Helen*
My One and Only. Plus a ripped-
in-pieces photograph: my sixtyish Pop,
smiling, his arm around a stranger.

My sister tells this story about Helen:
She called, out of the blue, to—as she put
it—enlighten Mom about Pop's infidelity.
She badgered Mom, *You shouldn't let him*
get away with this—not from remorse
or shame but because Pop dumped her
for someone else. Mom and Helen
met at the Blarney Stone; more shots
of more vacations were tossed on the table.

Pop never took Mom out. I knew why:
by her early forties she was a mess—
few teeth, fat, dull-faced, stringy
hair, stained housedresses and the stuck
smile that appeared whenever she was
faced with a nonfamily social situation.
Helen—trim, smartly dressed, blonde

bouffant—looked like a lady who
a guy could show off to his friends.

There was a time when Pop took
me lots of places. He'd brag,
to waitresses and bus drivers, *She's*
my baby. But the year I turned twelve
our trips together stopped; he began
leaving us on Fridays. Never said
when he'd be back, but ten bucks
under the stack of plates meant Sunday,
fifty meant we'd see him in a week.

II.

Pop and Helen's pose reminds me
of a photo once kept beside my bed:
my married lover and me on the porch
of a fancy B&B outside Chicago.
I spent twenty hours on Greyhound
to join him on his business trip.
Big smiles on our faces but later,
while drinking champagne, he confessed
he'd decided not to leave his wife and son.

His nightly calls home always
ended with *love you too,* but then
he'd turn and swear he loved me more
than anyone else. I pitied his wife;
poor fool, if she knew the truth,
she'd be brokenhearted, maybe—he said—

hurt him by keeping him from his son.
Someday, I thought, we'll start
a family then he'll forget about them.

We'd go months without seeing
each other. My life became a countdown
to the next time. Then, for as short
as three days, as long as two weeks,
we'd stay in hotels, eat all our meals
in restaurants, rent sports cars, stay
out late clubbing, and have no-holds-barred
sex. Strangers mistook us for husband and wife;
no one we knew, knew about us.

He changed jobs and stopped traveling.
We spoke most weekdays, between eight and five.
I heard they: bought a new home,
took in a stray dog, went to Paris
for their anniversary, watched TV in bed.
Once I called close to five,
after an accident that totaled my car.
He cut me short because he wanted
to be on time for his son's track meet.

III.

Did Helen visit Pop during his final
hospital stay? Mom took a bus
there every day and sat silently next to
his bed until visiting hours ended.
She was stupid; hadn't he made

it clear he didn't love her? When I
visited him, he introduced me
to the staff as *his baby,* which made
me blush. We didn't talk much otherwise.

The hospital called Mom at 3 a.m.
They'd been married for forty-seven
years. At the wake she referred to him
as *Sam,* which shocked me since I'd
never heard them call each other
anything but Mom and Pop. Her use
of his real name implied a relationship
that was different from my idea of it.
But she said nothing more about them.

IV.

My lover didn't call. Two weeks passed.
The message on his work number told me
he was out of the office. I left
messages and considered calling his home.
Turned out he'd sprained his back
and couldn't call because his wife
would've had to dial the phone for him.
I realized that no one would know
to tell him if something happened to me.

Our affair lasted four years.
The final straw: my pregnancy scare.
Here was his chance to start fresh.
He'd give up one child but have another.

The divorce might be rough but,
in the end, we'd be together. Wasn't that
what we both wanted? He made it
clear if I chose to have a child
then I was on my own.

V.

Mom—who never told anyone, anything—
told my sister about the call; the two
of them went to the Blarney Stone.
As we look at the photo, my sister
tells me: *Funny thing . . . Helen looked
like a cleaned-up version of Mom.*
My lover once showed me a photo
of his wife: short, dark-haired, cute.
She looked, except a bit fatter, like me.

Between Marriages

Since married lover #3 chain-smoked,
I blew off twelve cold-turkey years,
and quickly escalated back:
two packs a day of his Marlboro Menthol Lights.
Since #1 drank Rolling Rock,
I started drinking beer
but #2 drank vodka so I switched
to Stoli-on-the-rocks-with-twist-of-lime.
I whittled down my food:
oatmeal and prunes for breakfast,
tuna fish salad on whole wheat for lunch,
mac and cheese for dinner;
after months a meal might change—
never all three at once.
My alarm, to fit in writing time, was set for four a.m.
though most days I hit snooze 'til six.
On managed-to-wake-early days,
I eked out poems that no one saw.
Yet on the job—phone company—
where my reviews had been some version of
Does what she's told but nothing more,
I now performed *above, beyond*
and got promoted. Twice.
Minutes after meeting an under-fifty man
my fantasies about him—sex and rescue-me—began.
The few vacations that I took
were rendezvous with lovers 1 & 3
when they went out of town on business trips.
No one knew about those affairs—

discreetness part of the deal;
I was well suited to such secrecy,
having learned, long ago,
the art of giving vague answers if asked
when, where, how, and with whom.
As for my family and friends,
I turned down invitations,
never said, *Come in,* to them,
let the phone ring and ring,
didn't reply to letters . . .
just couldn't think of things to say.
Window gates, cracks, leaks, clogs, and twenty cats
took over my home.

The Art of Restoration

Presume not that I am the thing I was;
For God doth know (so shall the world perceive)
That I have turned away my former self;
So will I those that kept me company.

—William Shakespeare

Summation

Snowstorm, two a.m., Journal Square.
Fifteen-year-old me, who'd missed the last Bergen bus,
huddled in the Glove Shop entrance.
No point in calling home for help—my mom sleeping,
my pop gone (who knows where).

The unlit streets too dangerous
in blinding snow. Better to wait for daybreak where
some signs of life in sight: beat cops,
barflies, lovers, and the lunchbox-toting-swing-shift grunts
who spilled from screeching trains.

The boy—about my age—ducked in,
bummed a cig, stuck around. Drunken mom threw him out,
no gloves or hat, had planned to steal
my pocketbook, hated when people wrote him off
as worth- or hope-less trash.

By five a.m. my cig supply
was running low; we passed one back and forth until
the filter burned. A cop, nightstick
raised, half-stepped into our space, *Okay in there,*
young lady? Yes sir, fine.

When the first bus pulled up, the boy—
whose name and face I don't remember—kissed
my frozen hands then looked me in the eye,
Little One, be careful talking to strangers.
His straight back turned down Sip.

One block from my stop to 111.
Trudged through drifts up to my knees but didn't fall.
No light left on in our top-floor rooms.
By then my face, hands, feet, and chest so far past numb,
I feared they'd never thaw.

In the Gardens at Versailles

Groundskeeper knelt before a boxwood row
and measured off, with steel straightedge, its proper
height. Snipped here, snipped there, remeasured then
inched on. Not even thoughts of footprints dared
to ripple the lawn enclosed by that green wall.
Across the way a twin row waited its turn.
Such careful symmetry throughout the plan:
where left side somehow always mirrored right.

We, from the top of center-axis stairs,
drank in how statue, tree, path, shrub, and guest
were placed just so. No broken limbs, no faded
blooms, and no part standing out—all snared
in picture-perfect web. As numbness spread
beneath my skin, I fought to keep my breath.

The First Signs of Spring

Because it was April
the tulip buds cracked then revealed
satin sheened blood red petals,
and the blossoming pear trees on Ninth Street
filled the air with bridal stillness—
the perfect setting for
the song of an unseen bird.
Then the woman in front of Balducci's screamed,
Adam, give me your fucking hand,
at the small boy with the dropped head,
his fists clutching his jacket.
I knocked her down, picked up the boy,
and fled up Sixth Avenue.
We stopped to get Toby, the ginger striped cat
asleep in the lap of a drunk on Fourteenth
who had scribbled on cardboard:
Toby and me are homeless PLEASE HELP.
I put ten bucks in his paper cup.
On the ferry across the Hudson
we tore the past off our skins
and threw the pieces into the river.
That night in my kitchen, windows wide open,
fragrance of hyacinths filling the room,
Adam and I laughed, danced to a salsa beat,
while Toby stretched out on a blue velvet cushion
and scrupulously licked his fur clean.

I Like Saying No

Pure No—straight from my source,
not diluted by *I'm sorry but,*
not tainted by white lies meant
to soften the blow or appease,
not shamed by the wish
Maybe she didn't hear it.
Genetically altered No
as indestructible as the roach.
Knife-edge No that cuts to the quick,
sticks in the hearer's craw,
rings in glass-shattering pitch,
flips things topsy-turvy.
Vitamin T No that inoculates
my self against invaders.

The Art of Restoration

She wipes off layers of dirt,
varnish, damp, and human breath.
Her critics argue these efforts do
more harm than good—result in mere repainting
that won't retain an echo of the past.

The decision: Be content with echoes—
or risk losing what's left, hoping to uncover
more truth? She hunts down accounts
of how the work looked then and then,
of what its former restorers did.
She analyzes bits of paint,
scopes out cracks with a Minicam,
dabs chemicals on tiny squares
along the edge where her mistakes
will be less visible.

Much preparation. When to leap?
Silver light spills through doorway. Now.

Watch. After months of stops and starts, her hand
trembles as it draws close to the Savior's face,
which has begun to breathe in time with her.

On First Seeing a Photo of My Mother Dated 1936

Long had I heard from others there were years
Your life was not the sad one it became.
Before your breakdowns made you feel ashamed,
You laughed, went dancing, dyed and styled your hair!
They said that '36—before the fear
Took root, before your mind went dark with blame—
Was best: you married Pop, your first son came.
I never thought those stories could be real,
Until I found the photo that you kept
Inside a box unopened till your death.
A summer day, you're sitting on the steps,
Your belly's big—it's close to Vinny's birth.
But here's what caught my eye and why I wept:
Your face was calm, so filled with happiness!

Revision One

In this version my parents' second child,
Louis, still dies in '39—a crib death—but
this time a priest, worried by what Mom whispers
in confession, refers her to a clinic where
the doctor doesn't say Mom's faking it
or treat her like a charity case. She tells
him everything—how every night since Louis died

when Pop's at work she sits in her rocking chair
listening for sounds from Vin who's two and how
she wears the same stained dress day after day
even when she brings Vin to the A&P.
He diagnoses severe depression but
tells her it's treatable with therapy
and drugs — not locked wards, not ECT.

In time the color returns to her face.
She laughs reading Wodehouse, bakes, puts on
red heels from long ago, quits fingering
broken rosaries, hums show tunes, learns to drive,
skips early Mass and, to her face, calls Mrs. G.
busybody-who-should-mind-her-own-backyard.
And in this version I am still the last of ten

but now Mom smiles when she hears my poems.

Dear Vicky,

Remember that summer?
You were eleven, me nine,
skinny bookworms already convinced
we were too ugly to ever be loved.
The mornings when my mother
didn't make me stay with her
I ran next door, up four flights,
knocked on your door, waited.
Sometimes I heard screams, slaps, thumps.
Sometimes I heard nothing.
Sometimes you clutched Thumbelina
and ran down the stairs with me.
Sometimes you opened the door a crack
enough to reveal the bare rooms within:
My father's sick. I can't go out.

Vicky, I knew, though we never talked about it.
Not while we sat for hours on the stoop
cutting out party gowns for paper dolls
and wishing we were Nancy Drew.
Not while we twirled in umbrella steps
up and down Belmont Ave.
Not while playing school, our favorite game,
or tossing stones on hopscotch squares,
and certainly not when we tied clotheslines
to a fence so one of us could double-Ddutch.

Before school started you moved.
My father found a new job.

We swore we'd be friends forever.
You never wrote—I think I now know why.

Dear Vicky, wherever you are,
I hope you met a kindhearted man
and had the family (one boy, one girl)
we both dreamed of having.
I hope you live in rooms of light . . .
I hope the beatings stopped.

A Note to My Future Biographer

When you write Chapter Four wherein you describe
my pathetic lack of housekeeping skills,
please take your cue from the *household* entry
in *Beethoven A–Z* which, after revealing B's sins
against order (little feeling for neatness,
apartment a shambles, meals at irregular hours),
concludes with this unequivocal absolution:
A genius should not be blamed for such conduct.

I'll understand if you can't use those exact words,
but don't let, I beg you, the full explanation be:
She was just like her mother.

Traveling Home on Christmas Eve

—For John

I've never had holiday spirit.
Before meeting you I drove around
on Christmas Eves to check out
decorated houses, convinced
if I was part of the family
who lived in a house resplendent
with cascades of white icicle lights, red
velvet bows, and lit-up plastic reindeer or Magi
or candy canes, then I'd know
what the fuss was about.

This year we're driving home
from a three-day visit to your mom.
Now eighty-five, she doesn't decorate as much
but still puts up a real tree, garlands
the door, and uses holiday china.
She liked the hummingbird sweater.
Your brother gave us homemade wine—
good mead, bad Chianti.
We ran out of things to say
by the middle of Day Two.
I didn't sleep well because we slept
in twin beds, separated
by a nightstand.

Three hundred miles
from Virginia to New Jersey.
After hours of houses covered

with blinking colored lights, the sight
of an unlit farmhouse startles me.
Did something bad happen to its family? Why else
no Christmas lights?

We stop at my sister's in Basking Ridge,
sing carols in front of the church
on the village green. Later we visit
with friends seen once a year.

Near midnight, fifty miles to go.
Traffic light, snow falling, too tired to say
anything but *We'll be home soon.*
Keep thinking about tomorrow's dinner
with five siblings I haven't talked to in fourteen years—
since Joseph killed himself.
Will they look the same?
Should I have bought gifts?

One-ten. Finally home.
No lights, no bows or wreaths, no tree.
No one but us.
Breathe.

I Made Fifty

despite the medley of uppers and downers
plucked from dealers' outstretched hands,
the Gordon's and Bacardi swigged from pints,
the front-seat sex with drivers who'd give rides
to lone hitchhikers, the near-midnight walks—
dressed in my Catholic-school pleats—
down Forty-second Street. Despite high-wires, gutters,
edges of cliffs, doors slammed and dead-bolted
behind me, the bus stations, train stations,
phone wires ripped from walls to end my talk.
Despite my refusal to ask for help, take words
of praise, stick to my guns, or leave. Despite
the untold number of times I thought,
There's no fight left in me.

Prayer

Lord, don't make me die the way Pop did:
inoperable the surgeon said then cut
him anyway. Ten lucid weeks
in a hospital bed. From day sixty on
refusing food to speed the process up.

Don't make my final minutes public:
women frozen in fire-filled windows,
the race car driver's crash replayed,
the journalist whose throat was slashed on film.

Don't make it like my nightmare where
the man who stabbed me, as I'm dying, gloats,
Now watch me kill your husband and your cat.

Don't make my last conscious day like Mom's.
Ten hours slumped in Emergency. No food,
no tea, her coat stayed on. Those last hours spent
with someone—me—who wouldn't even hold her hand.

And I don't want to die a suicide.
Don't want, the way my brother did, to pick a night
then have to figure out a way to move,
without a car, ninety-one pounds of chains
and blocks, eight miles from home to river's edge.

Lord, here's what I want: a private death.
Let me, like the decomposing cat we found
behind the backyard bush, die in a hidden spot.

Make it quick—the way the expert described
what happened to the people on the plane:
A light shut off. Take me by surprise—
bolt, brick, crash, or in my sleep. Let it happen
when I still want to live.

Watching John's Heart

Park roof-level, race back to ER
where John's hooked up to machines that track
the jagged-but-stable peaks of his heart.
His arm cuff auto-inflates;
red numbers flicker like crazy slots
until 70 & 120 win.
He, ever the scientist, explains:
systolic contracted, diastolic relaxed.
Sublingual vasodilator kicks in.
EKG fine, pressure fine, take a deep breath for me . . .

On-call GP shows chart to specialist:
more questions, more blood, more tests,
more blood, more results, more consultations.
John shows me how, with biofeedback,
his heart rate can be changed from scared to calm.
Emerson's Essays open on my lap
but my eyes glued to the screens. He shakes
his arm, the peaks go nuts. A nurse
appears in seconds, looks him in the eye,
straightens the sheet, and leaves without a word.

Subforms of creatine kinase found.
Orderlies wheel him to CCU.
Blood taken hourly through the night,
vitals monitored 24/7, surgeons—trailed by
their followers—sweep in and out of the ward.

No one knows exactly what's wrong until dye reveals
a blocked anterior descending artery.
The interventional cardiologist shrugs:
The minute I saw John's face I knew
something had happened to his heart.

John watches pictures of his black-and-white heart
as they snake a stent to the blockage site.
Later we laugh at heart attack jokes
while nurses lift the small sand-weighted bag
off his groin. Blood pressure numbers drop.
How do you feel? OK.
The numbers steadily drop. *You still OK?*
The numbers seem impossibly low.
One nurse, inches away from his face, keeps asking.
The other prepares an adrenaline shot. I leave.

By the time we're handed YOUR FOLLOW-UP CARE
with its list of *Call physician right now* signs,
he wants to go home so badly but
a part of me wants him to stay
where nurses and machines can keep an eye on him,
where doctors can diagnose, order tests, do procedures STAT,
where blood and screens and charts and the clues
that those in the know can find in a face
prove better ways than any I possess of finding out
what's really going on inside John's heart.

Reincarnation

As member of the Ailanthus clan
I'll stake my claim where other types of trees
refuse to grow—tenements, train tracks, cracks
in the Palisades, the used-to-be-full-for-three-shifts lot.
I won't care if my twigs are weak, my flowers
make some sneeze, my poisonous stems preclude
a food-chain spot. I'll take my place, with pride,
among beautiful-yet-unwanted common life:
gypsy moths, pigeons, thistles, feral cats.
When gardeners sneer *invasive pest* while cutting
down my trunk, I'll shrug and use their scorn
to feed my roots; so, even as they're gloating
good riddance to that trash, new suckers will
start breaking through their weed-free-but-dull ground.

The Road to the River Blocked

I heard the owl scream and the crickets cry.
Did not you speak?

—William Shakespeare

In Memoriam

So many mornings I have crossed
the quiet river where they found
your corpse and strained to hear a sound
you left behind. Is your voice lost?

A photo in the folder marked
Case 1460 caught your drowned
lips wide apart. Fish bites had bound
your tongue. Your silence is pitch-dark.

What if, against the water's seal,
I pressed my ear? Does it still hold
the ghost of your last sound? I'm told
some want such sounds to stay concealed.

But if I could I'd free your cry
and let its anguish flood my mouth
until, now knowing why, I'd shout
the reasons you preferred to die.

The Road to the River Blocked

I.

The rough X drawn above HARRISON REACH
(Report 2, see Attachment 3, L 10)
marks where the JFK Fire Boat dragged
completely dressed advanced state of decomp
John Doe then placed you in a wastebasket
and cut the chain around your chest—this freed,
as noted on Page 2, the cinder blocks.
Detective H took photos, G bagged coins
found in your pants, while N wrote up the scene.
At 1530 the Essex ME
made her pronouncement. Eighteen years have passed
and chain-link cuts off access to the bank.
NO TRESPASSING warn skull-and-crossboned signs.
I kick the fence. A guard dog barks and barks.

II.

This fence, unforeseen, keeps me from where they laid
human remains while they began their search
for who you were, the way you died, and when.
Please understand how all those years I told myself
you were still waiting at that spot
and when I got there you'd explain the chains,
locks, bridge, river, and *torn into several pieces*
Medicare card. The list of disconnected facts,
like filings beneath a magnet made of sense,

would settle in neat lines of narrative:
event 13 from '86 fit *locks*
or night in '45 jump right to *torn*.
What's missing from the PM could come out—
I just had to stand on X; you just had to speak.

III.

Lucky for me: your X, because you floated
mid-Passaic, crossed town and county lines.
Their four reports tell same tale, different parts.
I piece together the two-month-long job
of naming *cause of death* and if foul play
played any part. They quizzed Castillo—he
prescribed your meds—and Ellen from your LKA,
which housed *low-income patients*. Last,
Detective N sat at his desk and read
his *narrative* to us—*known family*.
Although we had a lot of things to say
we had no words of yours that might explain.
The case was soon x'd *closed*. Eighteen years passed
before we found three notes in your effects.

IV.

Not much to go on. Three handwritten notes.
Unstained by coffee. Never sent. Not really
suicide notes. Written some time before.
Responses to unknown-to-me events.
One to our parents—here called *Sam & Joan*—

and one to each of two brothers. Three *please*
accept my apologies (for unspecified
disturbances in roles of son, housemate,
employee of our brother's painting business).
Three promises to *improve my behavior if*
I return home. Three *hope you understand,*
sincerely, Joseph Lamphier—which
sounds like too formal a way to end notes meant
to patch things up after a family fight.

V.

Let's say you had a fight with Brother K
who bitched about the crap piled in your room
and demanded that you fix things now, his way.
You rambled on about the rights of man.
The dispute traveled downstairs to the kitchen
where Sam, whose short fuse welcomed any match,
joined in and tagged you *nut case, son of a bitch,*
disgrace to family and wished you out.
Then Brother V showed up, spat his two cents—
his customers complained about your smell.
Joan clutched her beads and came to your defense
(you needed a nap, a piece of fruit, or tea).
Yet don't be fooled, it may not mean a thing,
my version of this could-have-happened scene.

VI.

That scene was someone else's, let's take one
of mine: on Christmas Eve in '82,

locked ward in Meadowview. You don't want me
to see your room. You warn, *Don't come again.*
I bring a brown bag full of gifts from Mom—
wool socks, new underwear, a flannel shirt,
and half a dozen navel oranges,
which you pick up but quickly throw back down.
How're things? Good. You chain-smoke Camels lit
by matches I possess and, per Nurse T,
patients can't have. While others mutter and pace,
you act as if we're sitting in Mom's kitchen.
The door near-shut I turn around and see
you tearing apart an orange with your teeth.

VII.

Trying to tear apart their open-and-shut
C.O.D.: drowning, Manner: suicide
has brought me to this broken-bottle lot.
Attachment 3 insists the riverbank
bends north one-sixteenth of white space past fence;
exact location of recovery
fixed there, not close enough for me to see,
and after all these years the road—unbroken,
no-name line on map—used by the cops
responding to *body found floating* ends
too soon. No sign of other ways back in.
Dear Joe, what now? I learned three notes and four
reports and my remembered-you, by heart,
and still your X remains unreachable.

Elegy for the Floater

Rest quietly, my brother,
the photos of your final
scream are buried in
a folder marked
~~*UNIDWM FLOATER*~~
Joseph Lamphier
and the box that holds
your ashes is sheltered
in our sister's house.

Other Books in The Laurel Books Series

Surviving Has Made Me Crazy
MARK NEPO

To the Marrow
ROBERT SEDER

Body of Diminishing Motion: Poems and a Memoir
JOAN SELIGER SIDNEY

Life with Sam
Poems by ELIZABETH HALL HUTNER
Photographs by SIMEON HUTNER

CavanKerry's Mission

Through publishing and programming, CavanKerry Press connects communities of writers with communities of readers. We publish poetry that reaches from the page to include the reader, by the finest new and established contemporary writers. Our programming brings our books and our poets to people where they live, cultivating new audiences and nourishing established ones.